a gift for

from

OTHER GIFTBOOKS BY HELEN EXLEY:
Go Girl!   Men! by women
The Great Gift of Love   To my very special Husband
The Naughty Ladies' Book To my very special Wife

OTHER BOOKS IN THIS SERIES:
A Woman's Work is Never Done
Too Soon for a Mid-Life Crisis
When I'm good I'm very, very good
  – but when I'm bad I'm better
Girl Talk!

Published in 2008 by Helen Exley Giftbooks in Great Britain

12 11 10 9 8 7 6 5 4 3 2 1

Design, selection and arrangement copyright © 2008 Helen Exley
Cartoons copyright © 2008 Rowan Barnes-Murphy
The moral right of the authors has been asserted.

ISBN: 978-1-84634-185-4

Acknowledgements: The publishers are grateful for permission to reproduce copyright
material. Whilst every effort has been made to trace copyright holders, we would be
pleased to hear from any not here acknowledged. RACHEL JOHNSON: From pp.144-5
of THE MUMMY DIARIES by Rachel Johnson (Viking 2004, Penguin Books 2005).
Copyright © Rachel Johnson, 2004. Reproduced by permission of Penguin Books Ltd.
OGDEN NASH: "I DO, I WILL. I HAVE" Copyright © 1949 by Ogden Nash. Reprinted
by permission of Curtis Brown, Ltd. GEORGE BERNARD SHAW: from MAN AND
SUPERMAN by George Bernard Shaw, reproduced by permission of The Society of
Authors, on behalf of the Bernard Shaw Estate. P.G. WODEHOUSE: from THE
ADVENTURES OF SALLY by P.G. Wodehouse, published by Herbert Jenkins. Reprint
by permission of The Random House Group Ltd. and Rogers, Coleridge & White Ltd., 20
Powis Mews, London W11 1JN.
PAM BROWN, CHARLOTTE GRAY, STUART AND LINDA MACFARLANE,
JENNY DE VRIES are all © Helen Exley 2008

Helen Exley Giftbooks, 16 Chalk Hill, Watford, Herts, WD19 4BG, UK
www.helenexleygiftbooks.com

A HELEN EXLEY GIFTBOOK

But It's My Turn To Sulk!

A MARRIAGE JOKEBOOK

ROWAN BARNES-MURPHY

A married couple are well suited
when both partners usually feel the need
for a quarrel at the same time.

JEAN ROSTAND (1894-1977), FROM "LE MARIAGE"

I love being married.
It's so great to
find that one special
person you want
to annoy for the
rest of your life.

MARRIAGE IS THE
DEEP, DEEP PEACE
OF THE DOUBLE BED
AFTER THE
HURLY~BURLY
OF THE CHAISE
LONGUE.

MRS. PATRICK CAMPBELL
(BEATRICE STELLA TANNER)
(1865~1940)

I married a General.
So I get dressed
Like the enemy
and he invades.
Works every time!

Jenny de Vries

My mother said it was simple
to keep a man, you must be a maid
in the living room, a cook in
the kitchen and a whore in the bedroom.
I said I'd hire the other two
and take care of the bedroom bit.

JERRY HALL, B.1956

A woman is man's salvation.
She is his past, his present and his future.
All this for just a few diamonds
and his unconditional, undying love.

STUART AND LINDA MACFARLANE

There are a number of
mechanical devices which increase
sexual arousal, particularly in women.
Chief among these is the
Mercedes-Benz 380SL convertible.

P.J. O'ROURKE, B.1947, FROM "MODERN MANNERS"

A successful man is one who
makes more money than his wife can spend.
A successful woman
is one who can find such a man.

LANA TURNER (1921-1995)

HUSBANDS!

There are two times
when a man doesn't
understand a woman —
before marriage and
after marriage.

AUTHOR UNKNOWN

Husbands
are like fires.
They go out if
unattended.

ZSA ZSA GABOR, B.1919

A husband is the bloke that sticks with you through the troubles you wouldn't have had if you hadn't married him in the first place.

AUTHOR UNKNOWN

I will tell you the real secret of how to stay married. Keep the cave clean. They want the cave clean and spotless. Air-conditioned, if possible. Sharpen his spear, and stick it in his hand when he goes out in the morning to spear that bear; and when the bear chases him, console him when he comes home at night, and tell him what a big man he is, and then hide the spear so he doesn't fall over it and stab himself....

JEROME CHODOROV AND JOSEPH FIELDS

All any woman asks
of her husband is that he
love her and obey
her commandments.

JOHN W. RAPER, FROM "WHAT THIS WORLD NEEDS"

A husband is what's left of the lover after
the nerve has been extracted.

HELEN ROWLAND (1875-1950)

No married man's ever made up
his mind till he's heard what his wife
has got to say about it.

W. SOMERSET MAUGHAM (1874-1965)

Compromise:
An amiable arrangement between
husband and wife whereby they agree
to let her have her own way.

AUTHOR UNKNOWN

The best way to remember your wife's birthday is to forget it once.

JOSEPH COSSMAN (1918~2002)

Marriage is the alliance of two people, one of whom never remembers birthdays and the other never forgets.

OGDEN NASH (1902-1971),
FROM "I DO, I WILL, I HAVE"

Marriage: A legal or religious ceremony by which two persons of the opposite sex solemnly agree to harass and spy on each other for ninety-nine years, or until death do them join.

ELBERT HUBBARD (1865-1915)

Before marriage she talks
and he listens. After marriage he
talks and she listens.
After a few years, nobody talks and
the people next door listen.

AUTHOR UNKNOWN

BRIGANDS DEMAND YOUR
MONEY OR YOUR LIFE;
WOMEN REQUIRE BOTH.

SAMUEL BUTLER (1835~1902)

Women should have labels
on their foreheads saying
"Government Health Warning:
women can seriously damage
your brains, genitals,
current account, confidence,
razor blades, and good standing
among your friends".

JEFFREY BERNARD (1932-1997)

It has been discovered
experimentally that you can draw
laughter from an audience
anywhere in the world,
of any class or race, simply by
walking on to a stage,
and uttering the
words "I am a married man".

TED KAVANAGH

A woman waits
motionless
until she is wooed.
That is how the
spider waits for the fly.

GEORGE BERNARD SHAW (1856-1950)

I never knew
what real happiness was
until I got married.
And by then
it was too late.

Max Kauffmann

I never married because I have three pets at home that answer the same purpose as a husband. I have a dog that growls every morning, a parrot that swears all afternoon, and a cat that comes home late at night.

MARIE CORELLI (1855-1924)

CHUMPS
make the best husbands

He's a chump, you know.
That's what I love about him. That
and the way his ears wiggle when
he gets excited. Chumps always make the
best husbands. When you marry,
Sally, grab a chump. Tap his forehead first,
and if it rings solid, don't hesitate.
All the unhappy marriages come from the
husband having brains.
What good are brains to a man?
They only unsettle him.

P.G. WODEHOUSE (1881-1975),
FROM "THE ADVENTURES OF SALLY"

WOMEN CRY AT WEDDINGS, AND NO ONE SEEMS TO WONDER WHY.

PAM BROWN, B.1928

In olden times sacrifices
were made at the altar – a custom
which is still continued.

HELEN ROWLAND (1875-1950)

Oh girls! set your affections
on cats, poodles, parrots or lap dogs;
but let matrimony alone.
It's the hardest way on earth
of getting a living.

FANNY FERN (1811-1872)

Among all the forms of
absurd courage, the courage of girls
is outstanding. Otherwise there
would be fewer marriages.

COLETTE [SIDONIE-GABRIELLE] (1873-1954)

Bride:
A woman with a
fine prospect of
happiness behind her.

AMBROSE BIERCE (1842-1914),
FROM "THE DEVIL'S DICTIONARY"

Fellows, Never tell your bride~to~be that you are unworthy of her... Let it come as a surprise.

Lee Laws

Every man who is high up likes to feel that he has done it all himself. And the wife smiles and lets it go at that. It's our only joke. Every woman knows that.

FROM "WHAT EVERY WOMAN KNOWS" BY J.M. BARRIE (1860-1937)

The average man expects to
get married as soon
as he can find a girl who loves him
as much as he loves himself.

EDWARD PHILIPS

He used to grab me
in his arms, hold me close
– and tell me
how wonderful he was.

SHELLEY WINTERS, B.1922,
ON HER EX-HUSBAND.

I THINK THEREFORE I'M SINGLE.

LIZZ WINSTEAD

If you want to sacrifice
the admiration of many men for
the criticism of one,
go ahead, get married.

KATHARINE HEPBURN (1907-2003)

One way to see less of a
man you don't like is to marry him.

EDWARD PHILIPS

SHOPAHOLICS!

No woman marries for money:
they are all clever enough, before
marrying a millionaire,
to fall in love with him first.

CESARE PAVESE (1908-1950)

There is only one thing
for a man to do who is married to
a woman who enjoys spending money
and that is to enjoy earning it.

E.W. HOWE, FROM "COUNTRY TOWN SAYINGS"

I had my credit card stolen,
but I didn't report it
because whoever stole it is spending
less than my wife.

HENNY YOUNGMAN (1906-1998)

HUSBANDS: A small band of men,
armed only with small wallets,
besieged by a horde of wives and children.

NATIONAL LAMPOON, 1979

A man may be a fool and not know it —
but not if he is married.

H. L. MENCKEN (1880-1956)

FOR SALE BY OWNER
Complete set of
Encyclopaedia Britannica.
45 volumes. Excellent condition.
$1,000 or best offer.
No longer needed.
Got married last weekend.
Wife knows everything.

FROM "NEW YORK TIMES"

If you want my opinion of these
matters — I don't think a husband can
ever be in the right!

JOHN VANBRUGH

A WOMAN KNOWS THERE ARE TWO SIDES TO EVERY QUESTION:~ THERE IS HER HUSBAND'S SIDE AND THERE IS THE RIGHT SIDE.

AUTHOR UNKNOWN

I said to my husband,
you must develop some
mechanical skills,
like getting out of bed.

PHYLLIS DILLER, B.1917

Deep down inside, men are
biological creatures, like
jellyfish or trees, only less likely
to clean the bathroom.

DAVE BARRY, B.1947

My husband never asks for my advice but he gets it just the same.

MARJORIE PROOPS (1911~1996)

The most happy marriage I can picture
or imagine to myself would be the
union of a deaf man to a blind woman.

SAMUEL TAYLOR COLERIDGE (1772-1834)

My wife and I had words
— but I never got to use mine.

FIBBER MCGEE

My wife has a slight impediment in
her speech — every now and then she
stops to breathe.

JIMMY DURANTE (1893-1980)

Battle Of the Bed

...the test of an accommodating
marriage is not loving each other's
friends and families as one's own,
making sacrifices for each other's
career or agreeing about education.
It is sharing a bedroom.
It must be vanishingly rare to find
two people who always agree on such
issues of global concern: duvet
versus blankets? Window open or
shut? Heating on or off?
As Leonard Woolf (I think) said,
the secret of a happy marriage is
to share a roof, but not a ceiling.

RACHEL JOHNSON, FROM "THE MUMMY DIARIES"

If you think women
are the weaker sex,
try pulling
the blankets back
to your side.

STUART TURNER

Modern drugs
are wonderful. They enable a
wife with pneumonia
to nurse her
husband through flu.

JILLY COOPER, B.1937

No man
has ever had
an ordinary
cold.

PAM BROWN, B.1928

Women Like Silent Men~ They Think They are Listening.

Marcel Achard (1899~1974)

If love means never having to say you're sorry, then marriage means always having to say everything twice.

ESTELLE GETTY, B.1924

How does a man yell at his children? "Honey, can't you keep them out of my hair?"

NAN TUCKET

One good Husband is worth two good Wives, for the scarcer things are, the more they're valued.

BENJAMIN FRANKLIN (1706-1790)

I have never married — I find that if I come to like a young woman well enough to marry her, I also find that I have come to like her far too well to wish to see her tied to an irritable bad-tempered old boor for life.

GILBERT HARDING (1907-1960)

The men that women marry,
And why they marry them,
will always be
A marvel and a mystery to the world.

HENRY WADSWORTH LONGFELLOW (1807-1882)

In saying what is obvious, never choose cunning. Yelling works better.

CYNTHIA OZICK, B.1928
FROM "THE FIRST MS. READER"

Advice

Give a man a fish and he eats for a day.
Teach him how to fish and you get rid of
him for the whole weekend.

ZENNA SCHAFFER

Marry rich. Buy him a
pacemaker, then stand behind
him and say "boo".

JOAN RIVERS, B.1933

The Japanese have a word for it.
It's judo – the art of
conquering by yielding. The Western
equivalent of judo is "Yes, Dear."

J.P. MCEVOY

I never hated a man enough to give his diamonds back.

Zsa Zsa Gabor, b.1919

When I got divorced, I went through
the various stages of
grieving — anger, denial, and dancing
around my settlement cash.

MAURA KENNEDY

Trust your husband,
adore your husband, and get as
much as you can in your own name.

JOAN RIVERS' MOTHER , B.1933

Never give back the ring.
Never.
Swallow it first.

JOAN RIVERS, B.1933

It is wise for all men to marry.
Those who find a good wife are blessed with
happiness. Those who don't are
blessed with a low golfing handicap.

STUART AND LINDA MACFARLANE

BY ALL MEANS MARRY:

if you get a good wife, you'll become happy; if you get a bad one, you'll become a philosopher.

SOCRATES (469~399 B.C.)

Arguments pro and con a man's rights to have more than one wife have been raging in Indonesia for a long time. To the claim that polygamy reduces a man's life expectancy considerably, the *Times of Indonesia* commented, "We are unable to conceive of a nicer way to die."

WALTER KANITZ, FROM "THE SPEAKER'S BOOK"

After you have
worn a dress
for about
two years,
a husband will say
That's Nice, Dear,
is it New?

Elizabeth Simms

Jealousy

When he is late for dinner and
I know he must be either having
an affair or lying dead in the street,
I always hope he's dead.

JUDITH VIORST, B.1931

I wouldn't trust
my husband with a young
woman for five minutes,
and he's been dead for
twenty five years.

BRENDAN BEHAN'S MOTHER

Because a man is unfaithful to you
is no reason to leave him.
You should stay with him and make sure
the rest of his life is a living hell.

ROSEANNE BARR, B.1952

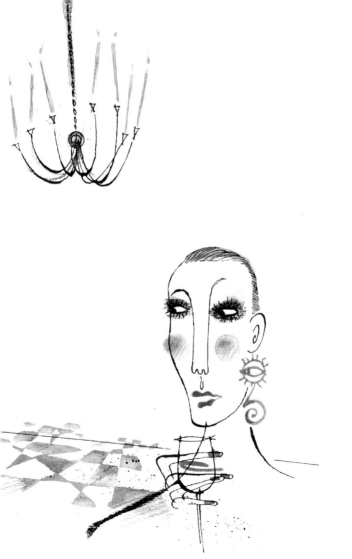

Women speak because they wish to speak, whereas a man speaks only when driven to speech by something outside himself — like, for instance, he can't find any clean socks.

JEAN KERR, B.1923

It begins
with a prince kissing an angel.
It ends
with a bald~headed man
looking across the table
at a fat woman.

AUTHOR UNKNOWN

I asked my husband to restore my
confidence. I told him my boobs were gone,
my stomach was gone. I asked him to say
something nice about my legs.
"Blue goes with everything," he said.

JOAN RIVERS, B.1933

Twenty years of romance make a woman
look like a ruin; but twenty years of marriage
make her something like a public building.

OSCAR WILDE (1854-1900)

A husband is...
the man whose eyes deteriorate just in time
to not be able to see the bags
and sags and wrinkles and blotches.

PAM BROWN, B.1928

My husband will never
chase another woman.
He's too fine, too decent, too old.

GRACIE ALLEN (1905-1964)

You can let off steam to
him and rant and rage,
and he'll look up from his
newspaper and say
"Did you say something Dear?"

ANN WEBB

He provides noble excuses
for doing nothing when household
mechanisms are doing likewise.

J.S. BARBER

My husband says he wants to
spend his vacation someplace
he's never been before.
I said, "How about the kitchen?"

NAN TUCKET

A husband is a man who
when someone tells him he is hen-pecked,
answers, yes, but
I am pecked by a good hen.

GILL KARLSEN

A husband says "I love you"
when you're wearing a face-pack;
and remembers your
punch-lines for you in public.

JILL WOODS

A husband is someone who
forgets your birthday,
forgets your anniversary, but also forgets
your grey hairs and wrinkles.

BETTY MORRIS

I love
every hair
on his
balding
head.

Iris Kestell

Love is not the dying moan of
a distant violin – it's the
triumphant twang of a bedspring.

S. J. PERELMAN (1904-1979)

Marriage is popular because
it combines the maximum
of temptation with
the maximum of opportunity.

GEORGE BERNARD SHAW (1856-1950)

Marriage advice for women:
The way to a man's heart is through his
stomach – but wearing
a flimsy red negligee will also help.

STUART AND LINDA MACFARLANE

H∉LEN EXLEY

Helen Exley is well-known for her
collections of quotations, with her giftbooks
selling five million copies a year.
Her books are on family, friends and love,
with a strong inspirational addition of
wisdom, personal peace and values books.

Helen has created strong selling titles on
marriage and love, with *The Great Gift of Love*
her biggest and most luxurious book yet.
"*But it's My Turn to Sulk* is the first
collection I've done on the impossible life's
task of living together", says Helen.
"My husband Richard and I have doubled
up reading the awful quotes to each other.
It's been great to laugh at the predictable
things that go wrong for all couples,
and us. I hope, like me, you'll find this
book both hilarious and healing."

Rowan Barnes-Murphy

Rowan Barnes-Murphy's cartoons are
wicked, spiky and frayed at the edges.

His fantastically well-observed
characters are hugely popular
and have been used to advertise a
diverse range of products such
as cars, clothes and phones,
supermarkets, bank accounts
and greeting cards.

For more information contact:

Helen Exley Giftbooks, 16 Chalk Hill,
Watford, Herts. WD19 4BG, UK.

Helen Exley giftbooks are all on our website.
Have a look… maybe you will find many more
intriguing gift ideas!

www.helenexleygiftbooks.com